Piano • Vocal • Guitar

Disney THE MUPPETS

Music from the MOTION PICTURE SOUNDTRACK

Disney characters and artwork © Disney Enterprises, Inc.

Fuzzy Muppet Songs
Mad Muppet Melodies

ISBN 978-1-4584-2134-0

DISTRIBUTED BY

HAL•LEONARD®
CORPORATION

7777 W. BLUEMOUND RD. P.O. BOX 13819 MILWAUKEE, WI 53213

Visit Hal Leonard Online at
www.halleonard.com

CONTENTS

THE MUPPET SHOW THEME

Words and Music by JIM HENSON
and SAM POTTLE

LIFE'S A HAPPY SONG

Words and Music by
BRET McKENZIE

Life's a hap-py song ___ when there's some-one by your side ___ to sing a-

long.

Straight ($\sqrt{3} = \sqrt{3}$)

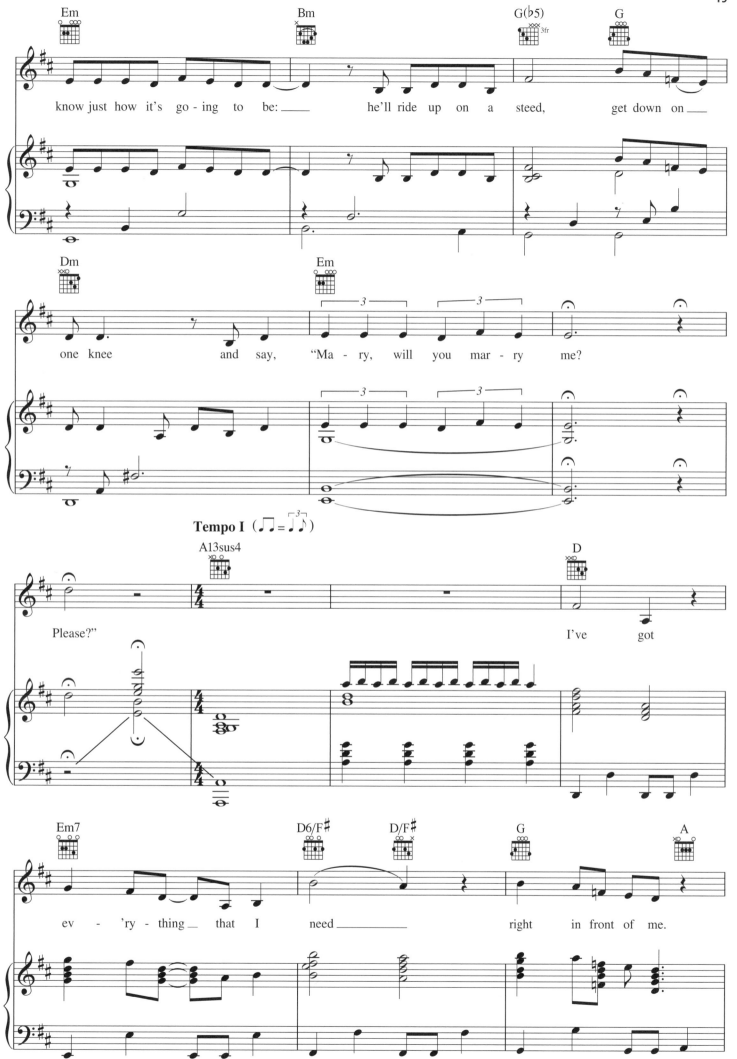

PICTURES IN MY HEAD

Words and Music by JEANNIE LURIE,
ARIS ARCHONTIS and CHEN NEEMAN

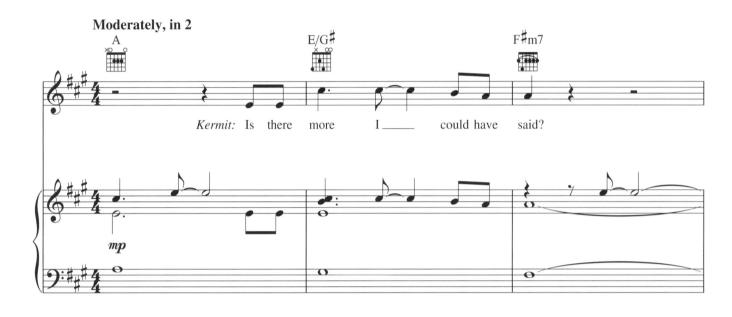

Kermit: Is there more I _____ could have said?

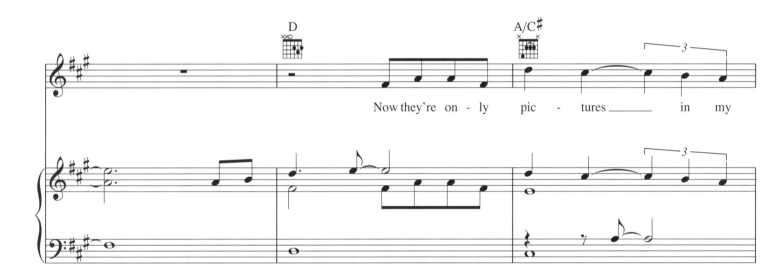

Now they're on - ly pic - tures _____ in my

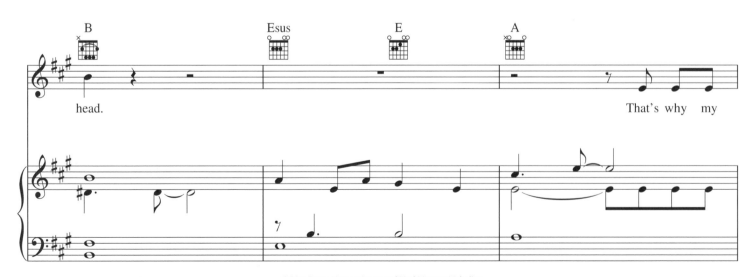

head. That's why my

ME AND JULIO DOWN BY THE SCHOOLYARD

Words and Music by
PAUL SIMON

See me and Ju - li - o down by the school yard.

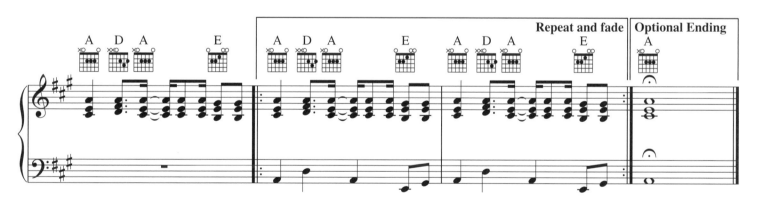

Additional Lyrics

3. In a couple of days they come and take me away
   But the press let their story leak.
   And when the radical Priest come to get me released
   We was all on the cover of Newsweek.

   And I'm on my way *etc.*

THE RAINBOW CONNECTION

Words and Music by PAUL WILLIAMS
and KENNETH L. ASCHER

WE BUILT THIS CITY

Words and Music by BERNIE TAUPIN,
MARTIN PAGE, DENNIS LAMBERT
and PETER WOLF

Medium Rock

We built this cit-y, we built this cit-y on

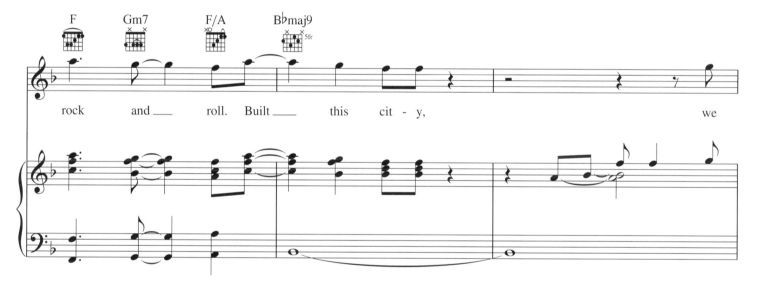

rock and __ roll. Built __ this cit-y, we

built this cit-y on rock and __ roll. _____

ME PARTY

Words and Music by BRET McKENZIE
and PAUL ROEMEN

LET'S TALK ABOUT ME

Words and Music by ALI (DEE) THEODORE
and BRET McKENZIE

Rap Lyrics

Rap 1:

I'm Tex Richman, Mr. Texas Tea.
People call me "Rich" 'cause I got mo' money.
I got more cheddar than some super size nachos,
Got cash flow like Robert has De Niros.
I use more greens than Vincent Van Gogh.
I make the baker bake my bread outta dough.
No, no, don't eat it, though; it'll make you ill.
There ain't no flour in a hundred dollar bill.

Rap 2:

Yeah, it's funny in a Richman's world.
When I need a piece of string I use a string of pearls.
If something's for sale, consider it sold.
I got so much gold, I gold plate my gold.
I even got a guy to gold plate my cat.
I don't regret much, but I do regret that.
If I could start all over, I'd do it all the same,
Except I wouldn't gold plate little Twinkles again.

MAN OR MUPPET

Words and Music by
BRET McKENZIE

SMELLS LIKE TEEN SPIRIT

Words and Music by KURT COBAIN,
KRIST NOVOSELIC and DAVE GROHL

FORGET YOU

Words and Music by BRUNO MARS,
ARI LEVINE, PHILIP LAWRENCE,
THOMAS CALLAWAY and BRODY BROWN

Up-tempo Soul

(Camilla and Friends:) Buk buk buk buk buk brrawk, buk buk buk buk buk buk brrawk, buk buk buk buk buk buk - uuuck. (Chickens continue.)

MAH-NÁ MAH-NÁ

By PIERO UMILIANI

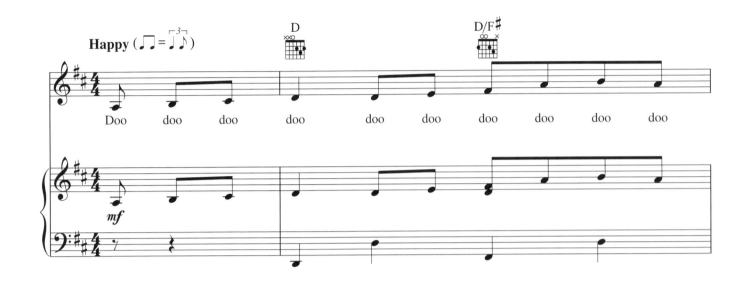

Doo doo doo doo doo doo doo doo doo doo

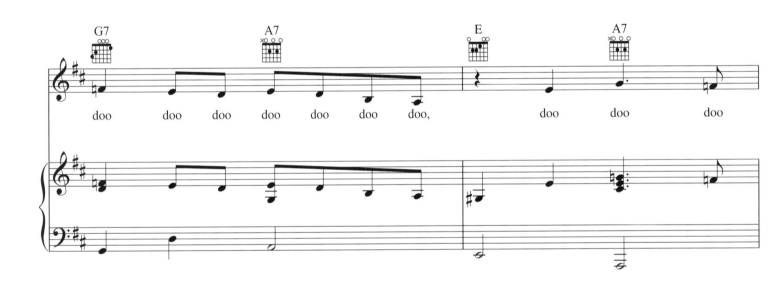

doo doo doo doo doo doo doo, doo doo doo

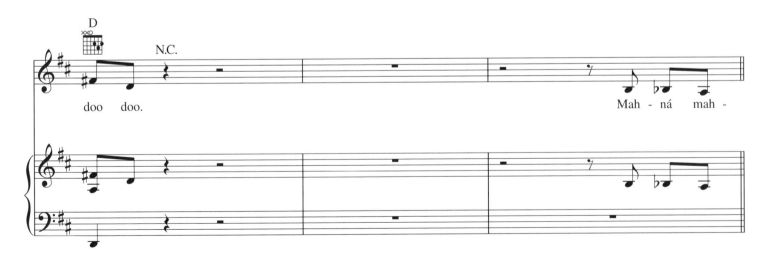

doo doo. Mah - ná mah -

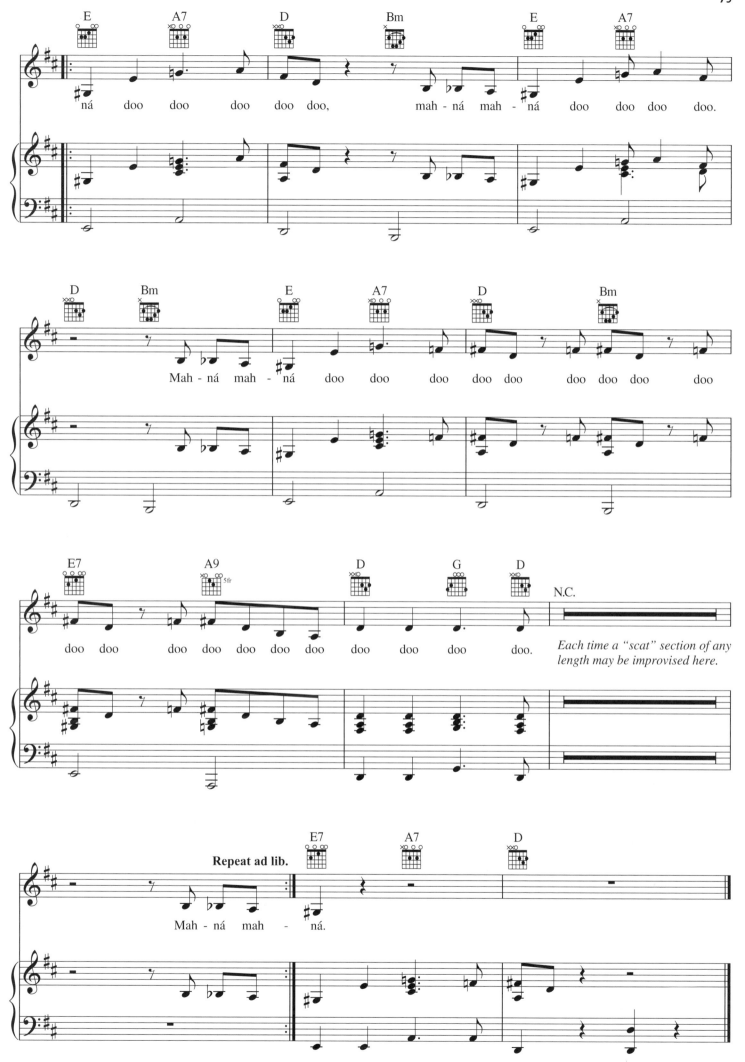